HANDCRAFTED AT SILVER DOLLAR CITY

HANDCRAFTED AT SILVER DOLLAR CITY

Home of American Craftsmanship

Crystal Payton

Photographed by
Leland Payton

Lens & Pen Press

This book is dedicated to the memory of Hugo and Mary Herschend who leased a cave in the Ozarks in 1950. Hugo's vision of a gathering of local artisans on the grounds around the cave was realized after his death by Mary and their sons, Jack and Pete Herschend.

Many people have contributed to the success of the Silver Dollar City enterprise but it's impossible to imagine the City without the sensibilities of Hugo and Mary. Hugo's respect for handmade objects and the men and women of the hills who made them and Mary's taste for traditional Americana are the heart and soul of the working village that is Silver Dollar City.

First Edition
Printed in Singapore

SILVER DOLLAR CITY ® is a registered trademark of Silver Dollar City, Inc.

Lens & Pen Press
3020 S. National, #340
Springfield, MO 65804

tel: 417/886-7124
email: payton@beautifulozarks.com

For other Lens & Pen publications visit our website: www.beautifulozarks.com

Typeset by Ross Daniels Payton
Designed by Leland Payton

ISBN: 0-9659983-1-2

Front Cover: Todd Nelson, potter
Back Cover: 17" bowie knife, "The Patriot," by Ray Johnson. Leather sheath by Rick Duckworth and Randy Morris

CONTENTS

SILVER DOLLAR CITY:
The Ultimate Craft Project

The virtues of the handmade can easily be seen. Wheel thrown pottery, free-blown glass, and forged iron have a purity of design that the manufactured object too often lacks. There is a tactile beauty to that which is born of the ancient marriage of form and function.

That a colony of skilled men and women work at traditional crafts in an Ozark oak forest seems natural. Silver Dollar City evolved from Marvel Cave Park, a nature preserve above one of America's spectacular show caves which opened to the public in 1894. Before that, a village named Marmaros was platted here. For a short time in the late 1800s, some of the trades we today call crafts were practiced on the top of Roark Mountain.

In the archives of Silver Dollar City is a tattered ribbon, a fragile souvenir of the first opening of the cave to the public, October 18 to 31, 1894. William Henry Lynch, a Canadian entrepreneur, owned and operated the cave with his two daughters, Genevieve and Miriam, for over half a century.

When Hugo and Mary Herschend first vacationed in the Ozarks in the late 1940s they befriended the Lynch sisters, then elderly ladies who still offered guided tours of the cave. Hugo, a Danish immigrant, and Mary, born on an Illinois farm, shared with Genevieve and Miriam an abiding interest in nature, antiques, and the values of hard work and self reliance. They were twentieth century vestiges of the nineteenth century Romantic spirit which questioned the industrial era's destruction of nature and traditional values. They found in the Ozarks an antique landscape and traditional culture less changed by the churning engine of industrial progress than most of America.

The Herschends, with their sons Jack and Pete, leased the cave and park from the Lynches in 1950 and began crafting an attraction that has become a romantic re-creation of an idealized American past. From the get-go it was a hands-on project, dependent on the vision and direction of the Herschends and the make-do ingenuity and practical manual skills of their indigenous Ozark workforce: Lester Vining, Bert Lewallen, Rex Johnson, and Fannabelle Nickel. Hugo died unexpectedly in 1955. The work of building from scratch went on. The tradition of in-house design, fabrication, and execution of projects large and small was firmly established in those early years. From the electrification of Marvel Cave and the construction of the cave railway, to the construction of the

first five buildings on Main Street when the City opened in 1960, every project carried the hallmark of the handmade.

Today, the park itself is a handcrafted masterpiece of American-style rusticity. It grew organically, the way a craft object springs from the unity of the materials and the maker's hand without preconception.

Mary Herschend and Andy Miller, former set designer for the *Ozark Jubilee*, a 1950s country T.V. show, were the primary designers of the City. With a workforce trained in antique skills, they made buildings fit the landscape. "Mary's contribution was intangible things," Jack Herschend remembers. "She couldn't tell you what she liked until you got it built." If, however, her aesthetic intuition told her you had built it wrong or in the wrong place, it would be torn out and rebuilt.

Mary's insistence that no trees be harmed is legendary. The park today is dappled by a thick and cooling leafy canopy. Hand built rock walls enclose wooded glens. Small clear streams trickle down the hillsides. Blooming flower beds and vigorous oaks flourish in spite of more than two million visitors annually. Antique and newly crafted blend seamlessly. The Wilderness Church is a genuine nineteenth century log structure; the schoolhouse behind it is recently constructed of logs hand hewn on the park.

The essential Ozarks is limestone rocks, clear moving waters, and forested hills inhabited by a people who revere tradition. The rides and entertainment imaginatively derive from local themes and materials. Silver Dollar City is deeply Ozarkian.

We had no architect, no blueprints. I think the City grew out of a little bit of everybody's imagination. We built by eye, no plans. It was a typical Herschend operation.

Mary Herschend

The railroads that first brought tourists to the White River valley ran on rails supported by Ozarks white oak ties. In fact, the region produced the ties that most of America's western railroads needed. Mark Edwards, Silver Dollar City's heritage craftsman (left), demonstrates the art of converting an oak tree into a tie or element of a log structure.

Working with hand tools was widespread in America only several decades ago. Myrl Evans, whose carvings were sold at Silver Dollar City in the early 1970s, carved the sculpture (below left) of his brother who supported his family during the Depression by chopping wood. A great many park visitors have similar memories of such early technologies as necessities. Silver Dollar City's experts in pioneer skills refresh these recollections and acquaint young guests with the practical aspects of American history.

Entertainment was a home industry as well in times past. Before the mechanical reproduction of music, every household produced diversions just as they produced their own clothing, shelter and food. Throughout the park are many live performances of this music. Some are lively tunes played to the exciting rhythms of a hoedown or square dance. In the Wilderness Church the old

hymns are played and sung. Just south of the church is the McHaffie Homestead, a log home built on Swan Creek in 1843 and donated to Silver Dollar City by Opal Parnell. There the Homestead Pickers (below) provide regular homestyle entertainment.

Porch music was an Ozark tradition. The songs could be 200 or 300 year-old British folksongs or Steven Foster tunes from the Civil War era. When the gramophone and radio penetrated rural areas, pop music was added to the repertory. Indeed, much commercial American music is directly descended from the English ballad tradition. Primarily it's played on stringed instruments. Hilarious or tragic in tone, the use of language is wonderful and expressive. Between numbers the performers converse with visitors, telling jokes and Ozarkian tall tales that may be centuries old, but still bring a chuckle.

Silver Dollar City craftsmen often use the park's themes as subject matter. The country bass player (lower right) was carved by Michael Kotz.

What I am proudest of is our presentation of Ozark life as it was really lived in the 1880s, and our revival of manual skills.

Mary Herschend, 1969

On the frontier, grueling work alternated with spirited "play parties" and lively social events. Our pioneer ancestors not only made their own houses, furniture, and clothing, they crafted their own entertainment. Today, organized on themes and promoted through the media, Silver Dollar City presents a new kind of play party, five formal festivals throughout the season.

The City opens each spring with World-Fest (opposite, below), a celebration of America's roots in many lands. World-Fest brings together performers, musicians, and craftsmen from around the world. Colorful entertainment for guests, of course, but also a time for City craftsmen to share with artisans from around the world age-old skills and new techniques and styles.

Early summer brings Music Fest (below). Visitors are treated to the talents of

nationally recognized musical acts playing everything from traditional ballads, commercial country, gospel, and bluegrass to zydeco and swing.

Two summer months are devoted to the National Kids' Festival (left). Acts and entertainment geared for the 15-and-younger crowd fill the streets and theaters. Autumn brings colorful foliage and the bounty of harvest time. The annual fall celebration, born of the original craft festival, offers a rendezvous of craftsmen from across the nation, from New England to the Pacific Northwest. Many craftsmen return every year.

Old Time Christmas rounds out the seasonal schedule. The buildings are draped with miles of twinkling lights. Park craftsmen create seasonal wares and holiday ornaments (opposite page) for gift-seeking guests.

Crafts on Park Today

Jack and Sherry Herschend, co-owners and founders of Silver Dollar City. Sherry's mother, Fannabelle Nickel, was a cave guide when the Herschends' leased the cave in 1950. Sherry and Jack were married in Marvel Cave in 1954.

We had started out with this season extension objective. Now, we thought, why couldn't this be our point of distinction as we grew? Thus the focus on crafts.

Jack Herschend

Interest in the handcrafted ran high in the 1950s and early '60s. There were other craft festivals scattered through the Ozarks, most notably the annual fair held at War Eagle, Arkansas. At these festivals craftsmen brought in goods they had made through the year to sell. When woodcarver Pete Engler suggested a craft festival as a method of extending the season, Mary, echoing Hugo's earlier plans, insisted that rather than just being a point-of-sale/retail event, craftsmen would have to show the process of creating their wares from beginning to end. The first three-day event, the Missouri Festival of Ozark Craftsmen, was held in October, 1963 and attracted 60,000 visitors.

Success of the early craft festivals clarified the idea of developing an active resident craft community. "That's what made it financially feasible to bring crafts in to Silver Dollar City on a permanent basis," Pete Herschend recalls.

As with the development of the look and the layout of the City, Mary Herschend's aesthetic intuition was the primary arbiter of the budding craft program. "When Mary saw an opportunity to have a craft on the park, she went for it regardless of whether it was profitable or not," Jack Herschend remembers. "Had she been a profit-driven person, we would have never gotten in the craft business." Under her guidance, craftsmen were encouraged to make what they wanted to make, not necessarily what sold.

Since the first craft festival, the primary requirement at Silver Dollar City has always been the ability of the craftsman to demonstrate. While recognizing that demonstration, explaining each step to an audience, is at best an inefficient means of production, it is the hallmark of the Silver Dollar City craft program. The act of creation—making a pot from wet clay, a multicolor vase from molten glass, an elegant basket from strips of wood—engages the viewer, entertains, explains, personalizes both the object and the maker.

But not all craftspeople are comfortable performing, answering questions, sharing stories with strangers. Often the process of creation is a solitary one and the creative person is an introvert, allowing the object to speak for him or her. As the craft program began to take shape it became clear that the City would have to find and train many of its own craftsmen.

Jack Herschend recalls: "The criteria for selecting folks was 'will they demonstrate in an interesting way what they do?' That was the toughest part. Most of the craftsmen who were really, really good at Silver Dollar City over the long period of time were extroverts that we taught crafts to rather than craftsmen who we taught to enjoy people. To take an extrovert and teach him a craft works. Taking an introvert who's a craftsman and turning him into an extrovert—it seldom works."

That program continues today. Ask any resident craftsman and, as often as not, you'll find a person who has learned their craft at the City after working at a number of other positions on the park.

The City has an internal program for the training and advancement of craftspersons: tyro craftsman is the beginning level. That is followed by associate craftsman, senior craftsman, and master craftsman. Each level requires accomplishment of defined skills and the creation of a certain number and type of craft objects.

Production continues in most crafts through the off-season. New stock is produced. Special orders taken through the summer are fulfilled. Craftsmen devise new designs, shapes, and experiment with different types. Crafts on park are not only re-creations of nineteenth century objects. Old craft skills are turned to creating objects appropriate to modern homes. Feedback from guests is a primary source for new variations like basket woven lamp shades and dog beds or handcrafted oak computer desks.

Once the park was closed from September through April, allowing ample time for resident craftsmen to replenish shop shelves. Today, winter production time is much reduced, from mid-January through March, and the retail selling season is much expanded, from April through December. As off-season time has shrunk and numbers of visitors has increased, the need for product has expanded. To fill that need and those shelves, the park now augments on-park craft production with products purchased from local and regional freelance craftsmen and from commercial sources for manufactured items made on a similar theme and with compatible materials.

The City has an internal program of awards and a system of recognizing achievement. Exceptional single items are judged by a panel of management and craft people. Those determined to be of a quality that could be "passed down from generation to generation" are included in the Heirloom Collection. The City also holds an annual "Craft Achievement Awards" ceremony where 17 different awards are presented. Many are nominated and voted on by the craftsmen themselves.

Pete and JoDee Herschend, co-owners and founders of Silver Dollar City. They met in 1962 when JoDee played Sarey Ellen McCoy to his Zekey Hatfield in the City's raucous street theater.

Demonstration gives a vitality. That is the ongoing difference for Silver Dollar City. It's the creative process and we (the audience) do respond to it.

Pete Herschend

BASKETS

Basket making is one of the frontier crafts that survived the onslaught of the Industrial Revolution. Strong, light, and useful, they proved surprisingly difficult to manufacture by machine. Hand woven baskets were the "carry-all" of choice in the 1800s. There was a basket for almost any task and the names reflect their specific uses: apple baskets, egg baskets, sewing baskets, gathering baskets, laundry baskets, etc. As the early immigrants to the Ozarks were southern mountain folk, the baskets they made closely resemble classic Appalachian forms. In the late frontier, basket making continued, an unbroken tradition. When the first trains and cars brought tourists to the region, handmade Ozark baskets became popular souvenirs.

When Silver Dollar City began developing its village crafts, the Herschends had only to look to the hills to find dexterous basket weavers. One of the first was Leslie Jones, who with his wife Gussie had a roadside basket stand on Highway 248. Leslie had no formal education, but he knew the craft of basket making from the cutting of the young white oak to the final weaving of more than 50 styles. He passed this tradition down to then-apprentice, now-master Donnie Ellison. Today most of the white oak baskets sold in the shop are made by five families of basket makers in the Ozark hills.

In the early 1990s, Silver Dollar City basket makers began producing a line of baskets made of cherry, black walnut, and maple veneers. While white oak splits are cut singly, by hand, veneers are thin sheets of wood peeled in a circular fashion from the log. Different woods are different colors, naturally. White oak splits are often colored with natural stains like walnut hulls. Other colors, blue for example, come from commercial dyes. Silver Dollar City baskets are never painted.

Through the winter, Al Kenngott, senior craftsman, and Kevin Pruett (above, right) work at the production facility weaving veneer baskets to stock the shop for the upcoming season. Apprentice Sue Schooler (below, right) demonstrates basket making for interested guests through the season.

More than 60 different types of baskets are made for the shop. Silver Dollar City basket makers develop new styles and forms often in response to suggestions of guests. Basket weave lamp shades, umbrella stands, even dog and kitten beds are recent additions. As Ellison says, "You can make anything you want to out of this oak. I mean anything. If you can think it up, you can make it."

Hillman, weaver, "a true gentle-man." Leslie Jones, mentor to Donnie Ellison, was master basket maker at Silver Dollar City for decades. He never learned to read or write but he once estimated that together with his wife Gussie, they'd made over 100,000 baskets. All were traditional shapes in white oak. He started with a young white oak tree, growing on a northeast slope where, protected from sun and wind, the soil is deeper and more moist and the trees grow taller and straighter. He cut the tree, shaved the splits, and wove the baskets. About basket making Leslie always said, "You've got to have patience."

Master of the white oak splits. Donnie Ellison came to the City in 1973, apprentice to Leslie Jones. He had worked with wood in his life but he'd never made a basket. The first six months he split white oak logs, shaping the wood and cutting the splits for Leslie. It's a true lesson, he still says: "You get to learn your wood. Your baskets are only as good as your wood." He's made baskets of other materials, cane, pine needles, even silver wire, but his roots are in the traditional white oak. "It's a beautiful grained wood, a close grained wood, and it's going to last indefinitely." Colored strips in his baskets are tinted by dyes, walnut hulls or mulberries, not covered with paint, which clogs the pores in the wood and makes the basket brittle. His original large swing-handle basket (opposite page) is made entirely of white oak.

Innovation in an ancient craft. Al Kenngott weaves baskets from veneers, walnut, cherry, and maple. He collaborates with other craftsmen to create unusual and appealing new forms, as witness the "vase/basket" (below, right) he makes with Bryan Keeland of the Pottery Shop. Both craftsmen sign each one. Randy Morris in Mountain Leather provides tooled leather accents to Kenngott's limited edition series of baskets. "When you combine two separate crafts, quite often what you end up with is greater than the sum of the two," Al says. The square apple basket (opposite), a perennial favorite, can be made with a lid and pie/cake divider, and can be ordered in different colors. "Demonstrating," says Kenngott, a former theater major, "is just like being on stage in the round."

WOODCARVING

Woodcarver Peter Engler (top right), in 1962, delivered a cigar store Indian ordered by Mary Herschend. Taking stock of the rising popularity of the frontier themed city above the cave, he ensconced himself in a corner of Sullivan's Mill, becoming resident woodcarver and founder of the Ozark Woodcarvers Guild. Pete carved out a prominent place for himself in the development of the City's craft colony when he suggested, in 1963, that presenting an autumn craft festival would be a good way to extend the season. He and Mary Herschend were of one mind: If you stay with the culture of the area—the music, the crafts, the history—you'll never go wrong.

By the time Pete left the City in 1984, Branson had become nationally known as a gathering place for woodcarvers. "If someone wanted to buy a wood carving, they would think of Branson," remembers Pam Gresham, carving coordinator and demonstrating craftsman. Pam brought a new style, chip carving, to the City. The folding screen (opposite page) is a premiere example. Built by her husband, Pete Gresham, and chip carved by Pam, the traditional Pennsylvania Dutch designs have symbolic meanings.

Valley Road Woodcarvers' Shop features the work of 60 carvers. Many are former demonstrating carvers who have retired or developed independent businesses and continue to supply the shop. As many as 40 or 50 of the carvers whose work is found on the shelves demonstrate their style of wood-carving in the shop on a regular basis. At the end of the year, the one who carves in the shop most frequently is presented the Dotty Award, a Ron Wells-carved caricature of him or herself.

Major styles of woodcarving represented at the shop are chip carving, relief carving, and "in the round" or fully three-dimensional carving. This sculptural category encompasses everything from small caricatures, to carousel horses and the enormous figures carved by Rex and Vicky Branson.

Northern basswood and butternut are the preferred woods. In response to the increasing popularity of woodcarving for the hobbyist, the shop also sells how-to books, carving kits, tools, and supplies for all three styles and all levels of skill. The Ozark Mountain Woodcarvers also sponsor the frequently sold-out annual woodcarving seminar.

Patient precisionist, chip carver extraordinaire. In the highly competitive world of professional woodcarving, Pam Gresham has earned the respect and admiration of her peers. Her specialty is chip carving, a Scandinavian peasant style of carving wherein the pattern is created by removing a precise, regular series of chips. She learned the value of minute measurements and how to draw geometric designs in childhood from her master machinist father. Beginning with small pieces—recipe boxes, napkin holders—she taught herself the craft. She pencils the design onto clean, sanded basswood ("it cuts smooth") and chips it out with a single small, short-bladed knife. Her work incorporates traditional Pennsylvania Dutch symbols as well as freeform drawing. She has authored three tutorial books on chip carving and developed a carving kit for beginners.

Pete Gresham, Pam's husband, does "relief carving" in which the background is carved away to reveal a design. Known for his mantels (below) and mirrors, he also built the large pieces of furniture like the intricately carved screen (page 22) and the magazine box that Pam chip carved. He and Pam both prefer what they call "functional carving"—i.e. carving used to decorate or accent functional pieces of furniture.

Pete and Pam came to Branson in the mid 1980s. Since then, one or the other has been a demonstrating carver on the park. They traveled with the shows put on by the Silver Dollar City Craft Guild and teach at the annual Woodcarvers Seminars. Frequently they combine their skills, with Pam adding chip-carved lettering or accents, as on the fireplace screen (opposite page) and the center mantel (below).

Four carvers create the carved and painted door panels: Pete and Pam as well as Pat O'Dell, known for her wildlife carving, and Dean Troutman, with his signature covered bridges and water mills. Custom architectural pieces may be commissioned.

Hillbillies have almost disappeared from glossy Ozark tourist promotions. They are a bit too rustic to remain poster boys for the fast growing and diversifying region. However, some Branson country music shows still retain a hillbilly flavor and Silver Dollar City guests find the hillbilly schtick of park performers hilarious. These skillfully whittled pop culture caricatures show pioneer Ozark hillfolks who can be easygoing (to say the least) or likkerred up and truculent. They are always singularly self-absorbed and self-confident. Derived from early literary accounts of the Southern highlander, the hillbilly image resists modern efforts to sanitize our legend of national origin. He and his backwoods kith and kin have bedrock faith in family loyalty and the primacy of personal conviction. Silver Dollar City carvers create these humorous caricatures in a multitude of sizes and guises. All sell well. A lifestyle founded on simple country pleasures and absolute independence remains tantalizing, if impractical.

Western motifs are well represented at the Valley Road Woodcarvers Shop. Historically, the Ozarks was a jumping off place for the Far West. The vast, arid lone prairie lay beyond the verdant, well watered Ozarkian hills. Texas-bound settlers often sojourned in the Ozarks before pushing on. Indian Territory was but a hard day's ride from the White River hills. The heritage of the West is second only to the mythos of the Ozarks at Silver Dollar City. Still today many Westerners vacation in the region. Mountain men, cowboys, and Indians are rendered in both comic and realistic styles by members of the Ozark Woodcarvers Guild.

Hillbilly caricatures like this woman of the hills (opposite page, upper left) by long time Silver Dollar City carver Ron Wells, are perennially popular.

Hillbilly incense burner (opposite page, lower left) is by J.L. Weathers. The smoke comes out of his pipe.

Bob Pester carved the man and his dog. (opposite page)

Western couple (above) was carved by Gerald Sears.

Indian with horse (left) was carved out of butternut by Dean Troutman. A park carver for 30 years, Dean is a frequent demonstrator also known for his water mills and covered bridges.

FURNITURE

An abundance of fine hardwoods, isolation from factories, and a shortage of cash promoted a vigorous local furniture-making tradition in the nineteenth century Ozarks. Many small villages had their own small factories producing tables, chairs, and cupboards. Indeed, plat maps of the original mining town of Marmaros, where Silver Dollar City is now located, listed a White Oak Furniture Factory as well as a pottery works. Wood products today remain a viable, sustainable industry throughout the region.

In the late 1980s, Silver Dollar City crews built the factory and found an antique power system and vintage machinery to shape the wood. Opened in 1990, Heartland Home Furnishings produces handsome, handcrafted furniture of solid red oak. The light-filled factory is equipped with an authentic nineteenth century line shaft power system and vintage turn-of-the-century wood working machines. The A. Dodds, Grand Rapids, Mich. dovetailing machine, patented June 14, 1887, is used for demonstration and for production. "Every drawer we make is made using this machine," confirmed master craftsman Warren Cook (upper right).

The line shaft power system came from W.O. Perkins Lumber Company, now closed, in Eureka Springs, Arkansas. Made to be powered by either steam engine or water wheel, the constantly turning shaft transfers power to individual machines via a tight/loose pulley system. Wooden paddles hanging from the spinning shaft move the belt from idle pulley to tight pulley to engage the gears. "In the 1880s, this would have been the basic factory set up," Cook explained. The line shaft could be run under the floor but that would defeat the City's mission of clearly demonstrating the "how" of what they produce.

Five men demonstrate furniture making during the summer. Warren Cook and John Gamble work through the winter to fulfill special orders taken during the season and to produce stock for the upcoming season. Construction of all furniture takes place at the factory, but pieces are stained and finished off park. The factory opened making only two items, a blanket chest and a barrister bookcase. Other items have been added through the years and they now produce bedroom and home office furniture, entertainment centers and accessories. Furniture is available in four different colors, natural, light, medium and dark. Most pieces signed with the dated Silver Dollar City coin are included in the Heirloom Collection.

Made of solid red oak and characterized by the use of raised panels on all sides, each piece is warranted for life. The jelly cabinet (right) is delicately proportioned, being only 15" deep, and comes in two widths (double width is shown). The single width jelly cabinet is only 18" wide. (Opposite page): Jewelry Armoire, in golden oak finish, has one cedar-lined drawer and a mirror inside the top. The Hope Chest, or Blanket Chest, is fully cedar lined. Both the Jelly Cabinet and the Hope Chest are taught in Craft College classes.

Visitors frequently find Walker Powell (above) turning wood as the chips fly at the steam duplicating lathe. Born in 1919 he grew up in the twilight of a fading frontier. His own roots are deeply intertwined with the history of Marvel Cave. His grandfather, Truman S. Powell, was an owner of Marvel Cave before W.H.Lynch bought it in 1889. Truman was also Harold Bell Wright's model for The Old Shepherd in his turn of the century novel, *The Shepherd of the Hills*.

The old time crafts at the City recall Walker's youth. "We had basketmakers back in the early days. And the lye soap—my mom made her own lye soap." Officially retired, Walker still returns to work at the lathe and entertain visitors with his memories of history of Silver Dollar City.

DUPLICATING STEAM LATHE

A steam-driven contraption of belts and gears held together by solid iron, the duplicating lathe still turns out wood products. Clouds of pure steam evaporate into the leaves as park visitors gather to watch craftsmen convert seasoned blanks of wood into rolling pins, biscuit and noodle cutters and other useful kitchen tools (upper left). Some off-park craftsmen augment the supply. Workers like Everett McGuire (below) always have time to explain the intricacies of this century old machine.

BISCUIT CUTTER

POTTERY

Before there was a Silver Dollar City, plat maps identified a pottery works at the mining village of Marmaros. When Hugo Herschend spoke of bringing together men and women of the hills to demonstrate their pioneer crafts, he included pottery making as one of those essential crafts. The making of wheel thrown, salt glazed stoneware persisted in isolated Ozarks communities long after that ancient craft had died out elsewhere. These nineteenth century wares were utilitarian, like whisky jugs or fruit jars, not decorative. Often, the only way early Ozark farmers could get their corn to a market was to process it into whiskey and haul it in jugs. So, the whiskey jug became an icon of hillbilly culture.

No creek bank can supply the clay needs of the City's Pottery Shop, so they order two custom blends of stoneware clay from a local supplier: a red clay with "just a little bite to it" makes the body of most of the utilitarian wares and a finer white clay that emphasizes the brushwork and shows detail better is used for the more decorative pieces. "One has iron in it. The other has very little in the way of impurities," explains Todd Nelson, master craftsman. "The same glaze on a different color clay body completely changes the color of a pot."

Once a piece is thrown, it is dried "leather hard," i.e. still moist, but slightly pliable. Before glazing, decoration is applied using clay slips, white clay to which different colorants have been added. "My work depends on the brushwork and the slips that I use," Nelson adds. He applies it to the greenware with brushes he makes himself (opposite page).

Then it is finished with handles and lids, trimmed, and allowed to dry completely which, depending on size, can take up to two weeks. Next, pieces are bisque-fired in an electric kiln which reaches 1900 degrees. After the initial firing, they are glazed and re-fired in a propane-fueled kiln at 2400 degrees. From pre-heat to final cool-down, this firing process takes four days. All stages of production are usually going on concurrently: pots are being dried, bisque-fired, glazed, high-fired or glaze-fired.

In the summer, every piece of pottery comes off the demonstration wheel in the shop. In winter, the wheel is moved downstairs to the production area and the potters work on. They produce pie plates, teapots, coffee cups, and show pieces, stockpiling for the upcoming season. With a nod to contemporary requirements, all pieces are microwave and dishwasher safe.

A master of clays and glazes. Todd Nelson deftly throws pots while conversing knowledgeably with curious Silver Dollar City visitors. He's been honing his craft since the early 1970s. "I like the Oriental feel of the bamboo and the grasses. When I was a kid I was the guy out chasing the butterflies and hunting down the bugs and bringing in the flowers and insects to science class. Now I'm finding those images are showing up on my work—dragonflies have been the latest thing." A fly fisherman, he not only ties his own flies, he also makes the brushes he uses in his craft. Over the decades his material preference has gone from "coarse, rough-on-the-hands clays to smoother, slicker, finer clays." The 19" charger (below) is one of his favorite pieces. Subtle, slip decorated hues softly fuse over simple, elegant shapes in his hand thrown stoneware.

A style of his own. Bryan Keeland came to the Pottery Shop after six years of summer jobs on park. After finishing his workday, he stayed until park closing, teaching himself pottery making. His persistence and determination impressed Todd Nelson who hired him as apprentice and has trained him. "A good thing about this pottery shop," Bryan says, "is they don't teach you shapes. They teach you the skills and you develop your own style." A meticulous craftsman, every mark on his pots is intentional. Inspiration comes from many sources but, he comments, "we add our own little flights of fancy." He makes the vases for which Al Kenngott weaves a basketry finish (opposite page). Size doesn't slow him down. The lidded urn (opposite page, far right) was made in four pieces and stands three feet tall.

GLASS BLOWING

Glass was a luxury item on the Ozark frontier, requiring a more extensive technology than home crafts like basket or soap making. Window panes and glass containers were valued cargo on the early steamships long before railroads and highways crossed the region. Only St. Louis, at the northeastern edge of the Ozarks, had the trained artisans and supply of suitable sand to produce utilitarian and decorative glass wares.

Jack Herschend invited O.C. Hammond, who with his son had a glass blowing business near Ft. Smith, Arkansas, to demonstrate his art at the first craft festival in 1963. With only a small oven and some molten glass, "They provided an exciting demonstration that everybody was thrilled to see," Jack recalls. Even with no finished products created (lack of a cool down oven meant items were broken at end of the demonstration), one couldn't help noticing the crowds of intrigued visitors hanging around the wooden platform. The unalloyed fascination of guests persuaded the City to open a permanent glass blowing demonstration on park in 1965.

In the glass trade, what Silver Dollar City has is called a "hot shop" where glass blowers make free blown or off-hand glass using ancient methods. Indeed, although the ovens are configured differently to allow visitors to see the process more clearly, glass blowing itself has changed little. A Roman glass maker from 2000 years ago could join Silver Dollar City craftsmen today. Czech glass makers visited during one World-Fest, sharing styles and techniques.

The ovens glow year-round. A reheating oven, the "glory hole," is kept at 2400 degrees. Two tanks, each holding 130 pounds of clear, molten glass, are kept at 2200 degrees. The third oven usually contains 130 pounds of a single color. Trays full of crushed, colored glass chips fill the tables at the front of the demonstration area. The glass artists roll the hot clear glass in those chips to melt colors into their creations. Wooden shaping cups soak in buckets by the tables. Sodden as they are, sparks still fly when molten glass is rolled in them. Everything made in a day is put in the cooling or annealing ovens (kept at 900 degrees), where it is cooled slowly over a 14-hour period.

Glass blowing continues to attract awestruck visitors. During the summer, two apprentices join the four glass blowers demonstrating the ancient art. Through the winter Dan, Terry, Ray, and Kenneth blow vases, bowls, animals, Christmas ornaments, and fanciful creations to stock the shop for next summer's guests.

Sculptor of figural glass. Dan Deckard, master glassblower, has been drawn to art since his Kansas childhood. Early on he learned drawing, watercolor, pastels, oils. Today, he designs most of the figural pieces produced in the shop. "Sometimes I sketch it, but mostly I just say, 'Let's see what I can do today.' And do something." Dan is the only one who produces many clear pieces. His focus is on always the form. "Color doesn't matter to me. It's just the way the material moves. If you're concentrating on the form, it doesn't matter what color it is." Drawing inspiration from classical pieces as well as contemporary ideas, like the crystal cowboy and horse, Dan makes the greatest variety of forms in the shop.

He trained all three of the glassblowers, Terry, Ray, and Kenneth, now working

the ovens. His teaching method? "Carefully and patiently, draw lots of pictures and bop 'em on the head once in a while."

The list of pieces Dan has had accepted in the Heirloom Collection is long. All four pieces (below) are included as are the two stemmed goblets and the lidded jar with fish on top (opposite page, below) Dan also makes the large blown glass angels (page 12) that have become a much-requested item during Christmas at the City.

American Eclectic, Midwestern Italianate: These are the words master glass blower Terry Bloodworth uses to describe his style. Terry came to the City in 1968 as an entertainer. His master's degree is in theater arts; his glass blowing training came from Dan Deckard. Signature pieces are his marbles, "one of the few things in glass men will buy, and women will buy for men," perfume atomizers, and paperweights. "I like the intricacy of working a small piece," he says. He strives to see how much complexity and depth of color he can get into a small sphere, no bigger than two inches. The reef fish (below left) was inspired by an illustration in *National Geographic*, then drawn freehand by Terry.

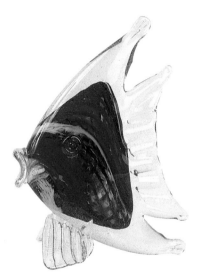

Against the grain, with humor. Theater-major-turned-glassblower, Raymond E. Jones trod the boards at Southwest Missouri State University with classmates Kathleen Turner, John Goodman, and Tess Harper. In 1973, he became the first singing bartender at the City's Saloon. Ray prefers to go against the natural tendency of blown glass to be round. He pulls and manipulates pieces to counter the natural shaping—making squared off perfume bottles or irregular bowls. His pieces often have a whimsical, fantasia-like animation, like the tall vase with its mouth pulled over (opposite page, center), looking like a plant that might talk, a character in an animated fantasy. Ray prefers bright, rich colors like cranberry red and iris gold, especially combined. He may top off a dark piece with an iridescent finish to add "shimmer and shine."

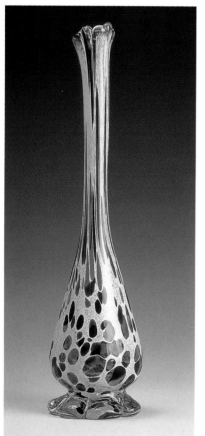

Balance, symmetry, harmony. Kenneth Marine, glassblower/guitar player, sees a similarity in the creative processes of making music and blowing glass. "You've got to have the foundational moves," he says. Dexterity developed in years of practice in either art brings fluidity, precision, and technical expertise. One whole summer he spent making Jack-in-the-Pulpit vases (opposite page, center) and now he doesn't have to think about the process at all, just the colors. "I let the glass guide me. The glass is fluid, it's always moving." Bowls (below) are fun for him to make. He cuts the rim of the hot glass walls and as he spins it in the glory hole, the bowl works its way open, the cuts adding flair and drama to the spinning colors. The polar bear is a Swedish design learned from a friend who studied there.

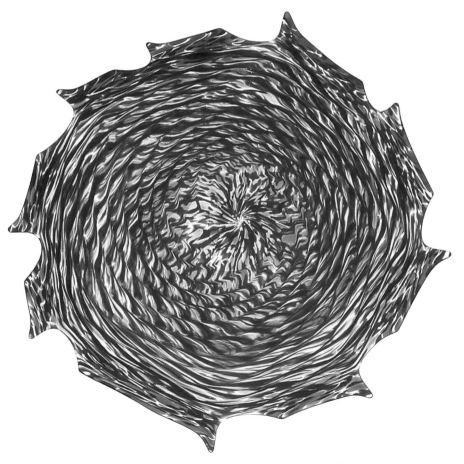

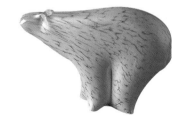

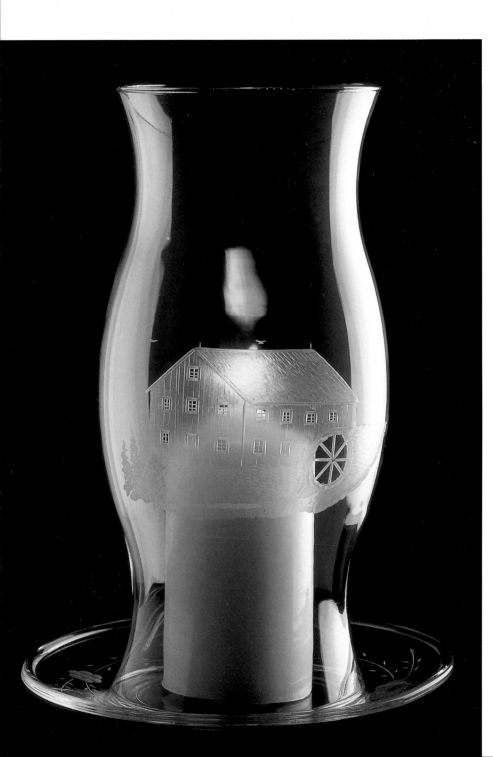

CUT GLASS

The very first thing master craftsman George Stiverson learned in his three-year apprenticeship at the cut glass shop was to cut a straight line. Next came the alphabet and the production designs. And finally, learning to cut on all the different shapes of crystal offered by the shop. "It takes all the three years," he smiles. The process he learned is called "gray cut" glass, using wheels coated with aluminum oxide abrasive in several sizes and shapes. From a waiting guest's initials to elaborate Heirloom Collection designs like the Showboat Branson Belle or the Wilderness Church, George cuts and polishes each one.

BLACKSMITHING

The ring of hammer on anvil was music to the ears of the men and boys in an 1880s Ozark village. The blacksmith's shop was a gathering spot complete with entertainment and the current news. While farmers, businessmen and friends conversed, the blacksmith made and repaired hinges, household goods, farm implements, tools, locks. From the simplest nail to the most complex tool, the blacksmith cast, bent, pounded out and riveted and-irons, lamp hooks, utensils and decorative wrought ironwork. If it was broken, he could fix it. If you needed a one-of-a-kind piece, he could fabricate it.

A blacksmith shop anchored the City's Main Street on opening day in 1960. There's been a craftsman at that anvil ever since. The legendary smithy of the City was Shad Heller (upper right). Vaudevillian, former circus clown, and all round performer, Heller *became* the smithy. Pete Herschend remembers, "He was a performer who taught himself the technical talk of a blacksmith and the foundry work. He was never the best blacksmith that we had but he was certainly good and he *communicated* blacksmithing."

The City's blacksmith shop stands in its corner of the square just as it was built the winter of 1959/60. Today's smithy, Steve Rooney, with occasional help from Harley Bearden (center right), pounds black iron at the same forge, demonstrating the antique craft for visitors through the season. The sound of the hammer still lures visitors to linger, watch, and ask questions. Unlike other "core crafts," there is no off-park production facility for the blacksmith. Winter temperatures adversely affect production. While heating black iron in the forge, the anvil cools and will cool the heated iron, making it unworkable. Sand that must be kept moist for sand casting freezes solid. So, once special orders taken through the season are fulfilled, the blacksmith shuts down until spring.

Visitors and photographers are mightily entertained when the sparks fly (left) but as Steve Rooney will tell you, those pyrotechnic displays only mean that the steel is burning. This goes to the heart of the matter: the commitment to demonstration. Still, as with other Silver Dollar City shops, the crafts dramatically pounded out here display tangible integrity. The spectacle recalls lines from Henry Wadsworth Longfellow's renowned poem, *The Village Blacksmith:*

> *And children coming home from school look in at the open door;*
> *They love to see the flaming forge, And hear the bellows roar;*
> *And watch the burning sparks that fly, like chaff from a threshing-floor.*

Producing enough hand wrought ironwork during the season to fully supply the shop would require more blacksmiths working full time in expanded facilities. Such a production system would be out of keeping with the 1880s theme of the City and the need for demonstration and explanation to curious guests. The City's blacksmith pounds out iron roses, candle stands, fireplace sets, architectural details and a dozen or more forms. And if a guest needs a special piece and can draw it out, the blacksmith will make it.

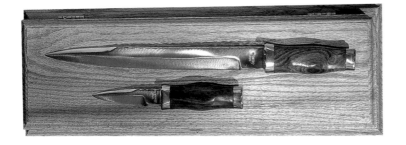

KNIFE MAKING

Ray Johnson, who has "built most everything that has a cutting edge," calls these edged weapons "man's oldest tool." Ray hails from the deep Ozarks country along the Eleven Point River. Twenty-six years as a welder gave him an edge as a knife maker. Ray's been creating a legacy in tempered steel full time since 1983. His blades can be forged of 640 layers of ladder pattern Damascus steel. Some collectors prefer rough-hammered carbon steel like the bowie knife. "They want people to know it's hand forged," according to Johnson. Every knife he sells he builds himself—blade, guard, and handle. Knife builder, yarn spinner, and poet, he sees his own place in the long tradition of blade makers. His poem, *The Legacy,* ends with the realization:

Quenched and tempered to withstand much strife
Can you call these Entities, just another knife
For long after their maker's fire has gone out
These Entities—these knives, will still be about.

LEATHER WORKING

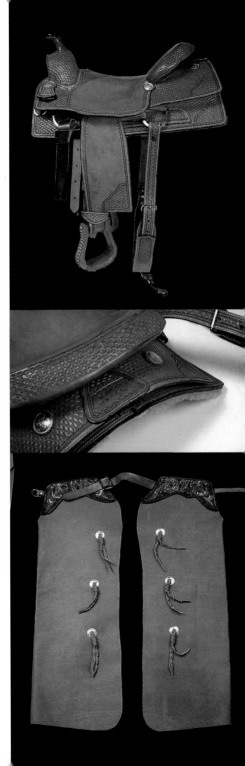

Mountain Fur and Leather Shop was a solid outpost of the Old West. But then the Ozarks frontier was a stopping off place on the way West. The long and rich relationship of Ozarkers on the lam to Indian Territory (just over the line in Oklahoma) and the Republic of Texas is recounted in song and antique acronym, GTT (Gone To Texas—usually just ahead of the posse). The first five buildings of the City itself were designed by Russell Pearson, who had planned and supervised the building of the very Western-styled Frontier City in Oklahoma City. Just as on the Western frontier, there were gun fights on Silver Dollar City's Main Street. The first entertainment ride was a stagecoach. The Ozarks' and the City's romantic attachment to the Old West was apparent from the get-go.

The Eagle Head coat modeled by master craftsman Rick Duckworth (opposite page) was a collaborative effort by Rick, who carved and colored the eagle and decorative patches, and Vada Swearingen (page 61) who sewed the coat itself. Rick's specialty is leather carving and his signature symbol is the eagle. While many leather craftsmen stamp the feathers of their birds, Rick actually carves each and every feather of his eagles. Color is dyed either by brush or airbrush using leather oil dyes. Fine details, like the eye of the eagle, are done with an artist's brush. The coat won Best of Category and Best of Show at the 1999 convention of the International Federation of Leather Guilds. It is included in the City's Heirloom Collection.

Cowboys and horses are as much a part of Ozark culture as mules and hillbillies. So it's not surprising to find that along with the chaps and belts, hats and vests, leather makers at the shop make bridles and tack. Rick Duckworth built his first saddle as his demonstration project for the 1996 Craft Festival. Rick's saddle has sold but Randy Morris's signed saddle (right) was new in 2000. Both saddles were included in the Heirloom Collection.

Production goes on year-round. In the wintertime they replenish depleted stock and research and develop new designs and products. Vada creates domestic items in leather: pillows, picture frames, lampshades. A pet new project is a line of numbered and dated teddy bears, "Vada Bears," made in rabbit furs and beaver skins which will be part of the Heirloom Collection. Rick has plans to make a double holster set on a wide belt with a whole western shootout scene carved on the back.

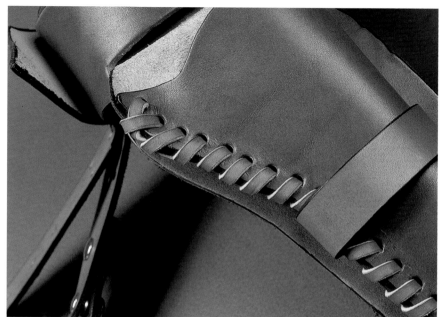

Each leather worker has his/her specialty: Vada Swearingen, (right) who learned to sew on her mother's old treadle machine, makes the apparel. Randy Morris (opposite page) does most of the basketweave stamping. He also contributes leather accents to many of Al Kenngott's baskets. Rick is the only one of the three who carves designs, with images drawn from wildlife, Indians and Western Americana. He taught himself the art. The rising popularity of cowboy quick shooting, like the American Gun Shooters Society, has made holsters hot. Hand tooled knife sheaths (back cover) and rifle scabbards round out the essential wardrobe of the man on the horse. Naturally, a guest can have a name or initials stamped onto any item made like belts or Bible covers (below). As has become a tradition at Silver Dollar City, many projects at Mountain Leather are a combined effort, using the skills of two or three leather workers. The rifle scabbard (opposite page, left) has both basketweave stamping and carved decoration.

Carrie's Candles, one of the first resident crafts, occupies its original home in the area once called Craftsmen's Alley. The shop makes novelty and scented candles as well as elegant tapers like those (above) held by Gene Bortner. Longtime citizen of the City, Bortner now supervises the hospitality of the McHaffie Homestead. The elaborate cut 'n' curl candles (right) are also made entirely in the shop.

CANDLE MAKING

Frontier homesteads were lit by the flickering flame of homemade candles. Each family made its own using tallow (rendered animal fat) melted in a large kettle outdoors. They were yellow, smelly and smoked. They had to be stored in metal containers so that rodents couldn't eat them. Paraffin wax candles were developed in the middle 1800s. They were white and burned cleanly but were expensive. "Paraffin candles were 'company candles,'" says Joyce "Cricket" Huth (above) of Carrie's Candles. Today, the shop uses paraffin for all its candles. Artisans work through the winter pouring thousands of candles for the next season.

Granny Clampett (Irene Ryan) of *The Beverly Hillbillies* hams it up over a kettle of boiling lye soap with Ethel ("Granny Two-Shoes") Huffman and Fannabelle Nickel, mother of Sherry Herschend.

In 1969 Paul Henning, creator/producer of the popular TV series brought his cast and crew to Silver Dollar City to film five episodes. The Clampetts had returned to the hills to look for a suitable husband for Elly May. Five episodes were filmed in a week. The City was the stage and its citizens were key players in every script.

LYE SOAP

Old timers swear by homemade lye soap—and for good reason. It's pure, effective, and costs next to nothing to make. Lye leached from wood ashes, lard, and water were boiled together for several hours in a big iron kettle over an open fire. Poured into flat wooden frames, the mixture would harden overnight. Store-bought soaps today start with the same ingredients and add lots of others to appeal to consumers. But Silver Dollar City's lye soap comes from the same old-time, tried and true formula. There's a certain mystique to its utter simplicity.

Silver Dollar City didn't have to teach Lucy Gold (left) how to make lye soap. A Stone County native, her family made and used lye soap exclusively until the 1950s. A true believer, she recites its virtues: It's good for your complexion, your old age spots, and skin rashes. It wards off chiggers and ticks. It'll grease a squeaky wheel or a sticky axle. It'll kill head lice and fleas on the dog. It gets stains out that nothing else will touch. And it cures the seven-year itch in only six years.

A GATHERING OF CRAFTSMEN

Since 1963 Silver Dollar City has produced a special festival in the fall, a gathering of craftsmen to celebrate the frontier lifestyle and crafts that are the myth and memory of the City itself. The first festival took place over a three-day weekend in October. It was then, and is now, "…not just a place you buy things. Guests actually see how people make things," according to Jack Herschend. A Silver Dollar City Picture Guide from the 1960s describes it as "the first wholly 'in-action' presentation of native workmanship." The second year the festival covered two, three-day weekends. Thereafter it was expanded to a ten-day event and now fills six weeks. Originally named the Missouri Festival of Ozark Craftsmen, it is now called the Festival of American Craftsmanship.

The success of the early crafts festivals prompted Pete Herschend and Don Richardson to mount all-out promotional campaigns. For a month each spring and fall, they took the City to its audience, bringing demonstrating craftsmen to regional radio and television shows in all the major cities of the Midwest. These now-fabled "dog and pony shows" also presented City craftsmen to the nation on *What's My Line?, Captain Kangaroo,* and *The Mike Douglas Show.* Those who traveled that circuit still tell the tales.

Many visiting craftsmen have long-standing relationships with the fall festival. Roger Sandstrom (opposite page) began exhibiting his elegant woodenwares at the festival in 1973 and traveled with those "dog and pony shows" to promote the festival. Sandstrom's treenware is avidly sought by collectors. "Treen" is an antique word referring to wares "made of a tree." He works with a large variety of native woods—lilac, redbud, mulberry, wild plum, yellow wood, osage orange, peach, grapevine, even poison ivy—shaping functional and extraordinarily handsome kitchen and pantry utensils. "Wood," he says, "is a substance with a soul."

Hugo Herschend had envisioned presenting to visitors pioneer crafts that were still a vital part of daily existence in the Ozarks. They were survival skills in a place where electricity had not penetrated until the late 1940s or early '50s and self-sufficiency was a way of life. These "heritage" crafts are part and parcel of pioneer life, and as such are central to the City's self-defined mission.

Cooper Doug Bratcher (next page top left) makes buckets, barrels, butter churns, and chuck wagon kegs from white oak. The "sampler" bucket he holds

is made from nine different woods. Designed to show customers the woods available, the sampler itself has become a favorite with decorators.

Gary Stull, wheelwright (opposite page, bottom), makes wagons for show or pleasure driving from the ground up, "from a pile of wood, to the painting, upholstery and pin striping." Half-scale wagons (in the background) were made in response to customer requests. One of his full-sized wagons was made for a brewery in New Zealand.

Horse-powered sorghum making (below) was a fall ritual throughout America a century ago. Rare vintage vehicles and antique technologies provide an amazing link to America's rural past.

Domestic arts shine in the fall festival. Visiting craftsmen add stained glass, raku pottery, and textile arts to the residents' offerings. Guests can't miss the clang of the warning bell, as raku artist, Brent Skinner, announces another "hot pot" is ready to be pulled from the ashes (opposite page, top). Brent first demonstrated his techniques at the City in 1992 and has since then fired over 10,000 raku pots for public viewing. Oxygen reduction and rapid temperature changes bring out unusual colors in the metallic glazes. More traditional skills find an audience every day. Kay Lambert (right) creates wall hangings and quilts on her treadle sewing machine. Sherry Bryan (below, right), the Ozark Broom Lady, sews and braids her multicolored straws into handsome and sturdy brooms for a multitude of uses.

Today more than 100 visiting craftsmen from across the nation join the resident colony for six weeks every autumn. The demonstration criterion still applies. Visitors make and explain their crafts to the thousands of guests. Booths for visiting craftsmen fill the Square and line the shady lanes of the City. Within the six-week time frame, some of the craft offerings change. Many of these craftsmen are freelance professionals who travel an annual show circuit. One booth may house two or three different demonstrations during the course of the festival.

Flawlessly woven Nantucket baskets (left) were brought and demonstrated by Deanna Savoy of Massachusetts. The intricacy of such weaving means that she may only finish one basket while demonstrating at the festival. Wade Sisk (below) smoothes a bow he is making out of richly colored Osage Orange wood.

Laura White (below) and her sister, Shirley Wood (not shown), demonstrate crochet rug making using a needle designed by their grandmother in the early 1900s. A deceptively simple technique, strips of loosely woven fabrics usually cut from old clothes, are crocheted into rugs and chair pads so thick and strong, "they wear forever." The sisters displayed a 45-year-old rug made by their grandmother. Genie Stewart (upper, right) brings her loom and elegantly woven apparel from Salem, Oregon. The craft is ages old, but her clothing has a contemporary flair.

Foot stomping, toe tapping, down home country, or earnest gospel tunes come from the Gazebo Stage throughout the season. During the fall craft festival, the haunting whistle of the ocarina may float above the fiddle music. The brightly decorated pottery flutes are made and played by Amy Lake (above right). Ancient vessel flutes were made from gourds, seedpods, bones, and clay. The modern 10-hole instrument was perfected in 1853 in Italy. Its shape and sweet sound earned it the nickname Sweet Potato when it became popular in the United States in the early 1900s. Guests may listen to a solo or learn the fingering techniques so they can play on their own.

Violet Hensley, "The Whittling Fiddler." She's been charming visitors at the fall crafts gathering for three decades. Her gift of gab and sense of humor are authentic. A native of Arkansas, Violet made her first fiddle in the mid 1930s. After rearing her 10 children, she returned to her fiddles in the early 1960s. Her music and craft have delighted national audiences on *Regis & Kathie Lee, Captain Kangaroo, The Nashville Network,* and *The Beverly Hillbillies.* Using native woods for the instrument's body, she personalizes each one with an etched flower or, if the owner-to-be is a horse lover, an equine profile. Every fiddle takes from 240 to 260 hours to make and is signed and numbered. She has made 71. "Next to my family," she says, "fiddle making's the love of my life."

THE LIVING CRAFT TRADITION AT SILVER DOLLAR CITY

Frontier lifestyles and technologies lingered in the remote Ozarks. Progress came slowly to the rugged hill country. Industrialization, of course, has improved the material comfort of daily life. Modernization, however, did not always improve upon the design or functionality of the traditional handmade object. Not only were certain manufactured objects less beautiful, but work itself lost much of its satisfaction. The repetitive nature of factory production lessened the pleasure of working with one's hands.

For over a century there has been concern that, as traditional culture declines, ancient skills would vanish. Arts and Crafts movements of the turn of the century were composed of idealists who often spent more time writing and defending their manifestos and justifications for handwork than actually crafting something. Silver Dollar City's programs grew more naturally.

Rick Crumley, Director of Merchandise, explained the continuing role of crafts in the theme and reality of Silver Dollar City: "Traditional American crafts with that special Ozark flavor are one of the cornerstones of Silver Dollar City. Hugo and Mary believed in this foundation which helps to express who we are and what we do. The Herschends set out to give guests something meaningful to do and see. Over the decades, we have built dramatically on Hugo's vision of recognizing the importance of American craftsmanship. Silver Dollar City is now truly the *Home of American Craftsmanship.* We believe there's something much deeper here than business. It encompasses traditions, attitudes, and skills deeply embedded in the old ways of the Ozark people."

Guests who visit the City share this interest in the handmade object as well as in the processes, materials and skills that create it. "Along with a love of what we're doing, we found that others, our guests, also wanted to participate in the rewarding experience of learning or mastering a skill," Crumley added. "For some, learning a craft, utilizing their own hands to express creativity, is a lifelong aspiration. Creating your own craft is very rewarding experience for the guest. In turn, we share the pride of passing on American traditions while educating people in an entertaining way."

True to its commitment to the craft program, Silver Dollar City has developed three levels of formal tutorial programs: Craftsman for a Day, Craft College, and Craft Seminars. Open to individuals of every skill level, occasional hobbyist to

full-time professional, the classes and seminars are taught by City craftsmen and nationally recognized professionals from across the country. The fees are nominal.

Craftsman for a Day

Begun in 1997, this is a one-day program offered throughout the City's operating season. Individuals choose a day that fits their schedule and a craft that fits their interest and come to the City for one-on-one training. Students are fitted in costume (at Silver Dollar City making crafts is a performance as well as a production), and spend the day learning the basic skills and history of their chosen craft. Students demonstrate for guests, and take home the craft object they create during that session.

The Craftsman for a Day program offers a wide variety of crafts. Besides the core crafts in this book, aspiring crafters can learn baking at Sullivan's Mill, take photos and develop them at the Tintype Shop, try turn-of-the-century printing at Madison's Mercantile, or pull their own saltwater taffy. "It's all about learning something new in the setting of your choice," Rick Crumley comments.

Craft College Classes

Offered several times a year, these two- and three-day classes, scheduled by the City, are taught by master and senior craftsmen in each of the craft shops on park. Besides the core crafts illustrated in this book, classes are offered in chair weaving, scrimshanding, and porcelain doll making. The Valley Road Woodcarvers Shop offers many different classes including Santa carving, shallow relief carving, chip carving, and hillbilly caricatures.

During the week-long Woodcarving Seminar in March, the Craft College also offers classes in a variety of other crafts for non-carving spouses and friends.

Craft Seminars

Multi-day seminars are offered in several crafts once a year with a variety of classes and skill levels. **The Woodcarving Seminar**, sponsored by the Valley Road Woodcarvers Shop and Ozark Mountain Woodcarvers Club of Southern Missouri, was first offered in 1997. Held on park in March, this week-long seminar is now one of the largest in the country. The most recent seminar had 35 instructors offering more than 40 different carving classes, from carousel animals to hillbilly caricatures, to 500 or more students. Many of the classes are

filled well in advance of the seminar.

The Basket Seminar and Workshop, introduced in 1999, is a three-day seminar in May with classes for beginners to advanced basket makers, some of whom make their living weaving baskets. At the most recent seminar 30 instructors taught students who had come from all areas of the country. Al Kenngott recalled that all 37 of his students opted for the natural woods. "They said they can dye their own material, but they can't weave in the natural materials anywhere else." Four- to eight-hour workshops offer students a wide variety of basket shapes and materials, from traditional split oak to Nantucket baskets, feather decorated baskets, chair caning, Shaker boxes or the pottery/basket weave vase.

"We offer a wide range of skill levels—whether one wants to learn the basics of a craft while dressing in 1880s attire and helping entertain on park for a day, or if one seeks to become proficient in the skills of our forefathers," Rick Crumley says. "Our craftsmen offer so much personality, professionalism, and knowledge that we wanted to share them. We started offering only woodcarving and, with tremendous interest from our guests, we continue to grow all our programs today."

Information on all seminars is available by contacting

Silver Dollar City   1-800-695-1353
399 Indian Point Road   417-338-8260
Branson, MO 65616   craftsinfo@silverdollarcity.com

ACKNOWLEDGEMENTS

Very special thanks to Jack and Pete Herschend, and their wives, Sherry and JoDee, whose unfailing enthusiasm for the crafts and the men and women of the hills has provided direction and constant support for the ongoing craft program. Many thanks to Lisa Rau, Director of Public Relations, whose enthusiasm and support were vital to this project. Members of the capable publicity and marketing team, Martha Hoy Bohner, Anne E. Ficarra, Carla Swanson, Nancy Henderson and Shannon Baker responded to every information and editing challenge.

Rick Crumley, Director of Merchandise, and Dave Pruett, Merchandise Operations Manager, generously provided direction and little known facts.

Deep gratitude to all the craftsmen who shared their time, creations, and explanations of their work, generously and unfailingly: Donnie Ellison, Al Kenngott, Dan Deckard, Terry Bloodworth, Kenneth Marine, Ray Jones, Todd Nelson, Bryan Keeland, Pam Gresham, Warren Cook, Ray Johnson, Rick Duckworth, Vada Swearingen, George Stiverson, Steve Rooney, Lucy Gold, Walker Powell, Everett McGuire, Joyce "Cricket" Huth, Roger Sandstrom, Doug Bratcher, Gary Stull.

Many others have helped, sharing their time and energy: Clydene Brown, Judy Miller, June Ward, Norma Jean Green, Loretta Martin, Karen Deeds, Sharron McCain, Patty Duckworth, Laura Allison, Sue Glannery, Jeff Kraft, Donna Hays, Lou Coil, Roberta Hardin, Karen Enno.

My personal thanks to my aunt, Mrs. Patti Crystal, for her encouragement. Her resilience and strength inspire us all.

PHOTO CREDITS

All photographs © Leland Payton 2000, except: from the Silver Dollar City Archives: page 4, Hugo and Mary Herschend; 18, Leslie Jones; 23, Pete Engler; 53, Shad Heller; 62, Gene Bortner. From Silver Dollar City Publicity: page 13, upper; 24, Pam Gresham; 60, Randy Morris; 63, Joyce Huth; 77, all; 78, both; 79, top two. Collection of Donnie Ellison, page 64, Granny Clampett.

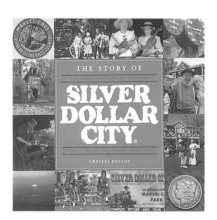

Read Crystal Payton's story of how Silver Dollar City came to be, and the remarkable people who created it. 128 pages with 228 illustrations.

Copies of both books are available from:

Silver Dollar City, Inc.
399 Indian Point Road
Branson, MO 65616

800/952-6626

or online: www.silverdollarcity.com